*Blood Party*

Merle Lyn Bachman

# *Blood Party*

Shearsman Books

First published in the United Kingdom in 2015 by
Shearsman Books
50 Westons Hill Drive
Emersons Green
BRISTOL
BS16 7DF

Shearsman Books Ltd Registered Office
30–31 St. James Place, Mangotsfield, Bristol BS16 9JB
*(this address not for correspondence)*

www.shearsman.com

ISBN 978-1-84861-414-7

ACKNOWLEDGMENTS

An earlier version of "California Again" was published in
*The Opposite of Vanishing* (EtherDome Press, 2000)
and of "Women's Pictures" in *As If It Fell From the Sun:
Ten Years of Women's Writing*, edited by Colleen Lookingbill &
Elizabeth Robinson (EtherDome Press, 2012).
An excerpt from "The Lemon-Scented Pine Cabinets of Childhood"
was published in *The Materialist* (2015).

# CONTENTS

Dedicated to "the Blood"
and their shining, injurious love

and for poet and dear friend Colleen Lookingbill
whose memory is a blessing

# Objects & Space (an Introduction)

In this room, says the Dharma teacher, there are objects – bodies,
flowers, chairs, light.
But there is also space.

In reality, space is all that is present.  And it's no big deal.

If you look into the night sky you will see space, and you will see objects
– the stars and planets.

Space is just the externalization of what you really are.


[Here is my photograph of
SPACE: ]

How much space do you occupy?


The other night I needed a flashlight and I called it: *fleshlight.*

That sounded right.


The Dharma teacher says:
do you really think you can *explain the universe* in five vowels & 21 consonants?

Laughter arises from the body-objects in the room.


Consider:

How much of your body is made of
        words?

The home language I never speak is thick with guttural sounds.

Inside this body, spaces.  Inside the spaces, memories.

Inside the memories, bodies.


And consonants.  And vowels.

*

A bird pecks the earth over a grave – comes up with seeds of memory –
consumes them and its wings and claw-feet bear them silently into the
tops of swaying trees

(and later, memory – shat out – crumbles back into dirt).

That's just one possibility.


I'm stuck with letters.

I – am a letter.

Everything made of space, including notes squeezed out of an accordion
or a bassoon.  Tempting; pleasing; the husks of words in voices digitally
present on my cell phone, for as long as I remember to hit "re-save."

But really, I –
am a woman.
A precisely gendered being with uterus intact, nulliparous   and breasts
   rippled where
small pieces have recently been taken.


This body:  one longs to smear it
  with memory – a rotted fabric    dank perfume   – stick fingers in the
     dirt mound on
the last, fresh grave –    taste

## Questions for My Russian Grandmother:

What beliefs are there about a person's soul before it enters the body?

How does the soul's entry into the body take place?

If a pregnant woman touches part of her body during a fire, will the child be born with a red mark on the same body part?

Should a pregnant woman not enter the house of a non-Jew or walk alone on a bridge over a river?

If someone strikes a blow with an axe on the threshold over which the pregnant woman has stepped, will the child have a harelip?

What charms, amulets, stones are there to give a woman power over the Evil Eye?

Florida: 1952

# AlbanyNewYork

How did snow

   smell?

        faint lavender
to match dusk's blending of firs in the *far-back*
 the children's yard

Hour of    the shadowcast

  *Our Home in Space:*


[  a lattice we called
the *snowball tree* ]



Mother
      Father

## The great *Blackout*:

It's 1965:

    Record needle bumps the disc's
far shore: drags, digs to a halt.

Reports of sorry office workers
packed in elevators
    leave a permanent scratch in my mind

: to this day I take the stairs.

Matches flare: it's hours till the power grids fire-up again
& he sits on my little bed's edge drawing circles
  with the tip of his cigarette

     father
         *daddy*

    How did it taste   inside the cockpit, face
grazing the glass?
–breathing inside the mask

The days of bombing raids inside Germany
  long done, your world
swagger & astonishment   big band blare Glen Miller
  lost over a violet sea

# The Lemon-Scented Pine Cabinets of Childhood

Stuffed pheasant perched on top
child's face reflected in door-glass
the world my parents made together and made meaning

whatever it meant to them
a child living there could only sniff or peer at
their solid presence

still in that room — doubling as *dining* and *family* because the house
was that small

– with the television on.
– with full ashtrays.

THAT'S LIFE (trumpet blare) *you can't deny it*

the way a dress felt on my mother's
body, lowered over her strapped-in
breasts, over the girdle (faint indent between
lower ribs, jutting out, kind of boxy

the portion of her body I saw often because
it was close to a young girl's height.

The way my mother adjusted his tie:

Fullness of that life: complete with garden peonies spitting ants and
neighbors at the back door bearing fresh-baked hermits and iced drinks:

[inside the spaces, memories;  inside the memories
   bodies
and the world that was theirs.


*


Writing: the girl, and the girl writing
fills notebooks, skins that lift words now
shriveling and the blue
ink beginning
its vanishing act:
at least two books per year (plus miscellaneous) since
age 13 and what to do with all this commentary, this
registration:


*Perhaps this is where you'll find your mother,*
sighing over the sink looking vacantly out the window or

dad, back from work with soiled hands, such a cliché, he wants to be left
alone in his chair to smoke, knock back a drink, the rooms of ordinary

complaint, veal chops, homework and downstairs in the basement office
the plans, midnight blue as your patent leather shoes, on the tilted desk

for a house that won't be built because the money's dried up, and empty
of politics (despite the thing called *Vietnam*, the thing called *Blacks* and
    *Rights*)

except for <u>Don't bow your head when they make you pray</u> and
<u>Don't kneel down</u> and <u>We're Jews</u> and that's the way it is (says crumpled

old Cronkite, so trustworthy in thick glasses) and *all ashore*
    *that's going ashore*
and *last call for Phillip Morris* —




My father used to say: "How very white of you."
It was a joke; it was a sneer.
What did he mean?



— something high-society, correct

  *not Jewish.*

# Women's Pictures

## Magnificent Obsession

*chaotic mouth interrupting rain*

A mountain waits at the top of the pass for slow-motion dissolve

while the couple in grey and     grosgrain
bury themselves in lavender

a darkening thorax surrounds them. His hands recast her figure in
sugar   for the thousandth time
   the *mise en scène* of love.     birds trill:

the smell of passion enchants the nearby villagers, out
for an evening stroll on uneven decks
carved of elephant ivory and caramel.

## Now, Voyager

if you find yourself aboard a cruise ship, then:

   cocktails – butterfly-gowns – gallants

offering to light your cigarette
(waves all the while bear you to a tropic coast, at night
the engines churning)

how grand to suffer wearing perfect makeup, *avec*
glycerine eyes
     your feet suddenly fitting

tiny shoes.   big shoulders, limp
hand waving protest
                  *– this exists in the dark. as it should.*

(while the ship all the while splits the channel)

the deepest Atlantic rift no match for what happens :


under the hovering pearl
of a lens
outsize features of a female face become classical

What is required? that the woman die
or suffer in a transcendent way befitting smoldering
light, sequins beaded in her dress, opalescent issue of
proffered cigarettes?

A gown burns

it must, her flesh
incandescent
on a darkened deck


imagine     a body designed
for love,     the smoke of it


  a sacrifice to keep us     content

## *Imitation of* Imitation of Life

All night thinking when I should have been sleeping or even just
dreaming in my pocket of warmth in a cold house, about her, soft
mutable face on which the play of expression registers through light. I
suppose only a man could have lit her this way; chosen her for the
shape and paleness of her face, registering as a blank heart amid
opposing banks of colors. The woman must suffer and deny herself, must
enclose herself in a wreath of stiff denials; must wear fitted tweeds
or *crepe de chine* and lady's gloves (and lady's slippers). And flowers
must pour into the car in which she rides, blind over the mountain
passes, heading into the lights of an old town under the wide-eyed moon.

\*

the familiar body of that woman (a bit short-waisted, not tall; cap of
red hair, voice careful, cream)

and the dreadfully handsome man

in one pocket a matchbook in the other a mirror

watchful, a child sore

from strawberries' hateful taste.

And how is it that she makes a place for me, for where I come from —
house full of lazy cigarette smoke, canned peas, raw
meat, a drink before dinner, a club, a yearning and a striving upward,
into a rarified life (I knew nothing of the one before), with all the
modern conveniences; with two eyes looking forward (a wandering one
    corrected), no limp
of an old-world name, all immigrant purged and the house looking spotless

We have a girl who comes once a week unlike any other family on this
street, she is a colored girl her name is Dot, no it's Dolly, no it's
thinking about that woman whose face blurs and sharpens containing
radiant confusion, and the cigarettes, the *capri* pants, the tastefulness of a
    well-modulated
tone (whether of voice or color or the way one thinks), but

behind floor-length drapes still you could
hear impatience and anger, too much spent on groceries, special cuts of
meat, the jobs that stain a man's knuckles, the woman as *fortress*
*home*, teaching her children politeness, sitting and standing, when to
extend a small gloved hand:

the costs of being oatmeal, taupe, beige (and yet the pungent
outrageous royal blue of our carpets!…. that *feygele* designer… but
how can he be a *feygele* if he's married? and his son, the handsomest in
my class, so much it makes me uncomfortable to be around him.)

And the woman:

blind, central, confused, penetrable

historic, momentary, fifties, white

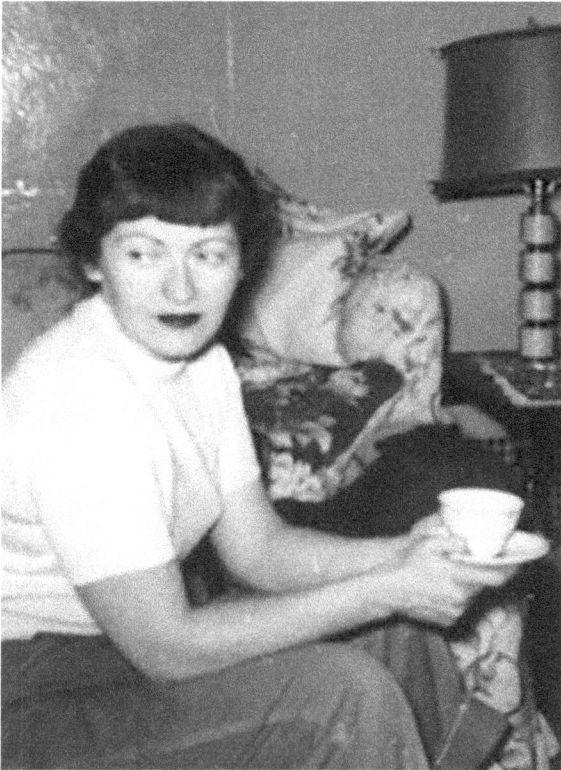

# Blood Party

Come hither:

a party at which everyone
now dead     converges on the dip: turning to display a new
ring, or point the foot to show the shoe or flick
an invisible scarf of perfume

over *gehakte lebn,* chopped liver, pickled herring

cocktails' tinkle & laughter & the smoke, creeping upstairs
& shimmy-shimmy music, Dean Martin, Nat King Cole:

*and a girl stays fastened in her princess bed*
*— champagne paneling, hot pink carpet —*
*reading The Lord of the Rings & waiting*
*for midnight:*

Oh — so long ago.
Heavy telephones corded to the walls

*Life* a magazine, with photo spreads of bleeding soldiers

and ads with women drawn in pointy bras, <u>Maidenform</u> something about
*gliding through a city night*

in my Maıdanek bra

# M

*//awaking — a smash of dreams.*
*can't reach the low-hanging fruit*
*it's all tightropes, recitation, a high yellow*
*meanwhile — that shadowy zone in which our lives play out*
*meanwhile — the rain pushed through & the hydrolics of each band*
*cause creeks in counties south of here to bulge*
*burst over bottoms, the high water mark*
*not yet reached. some cars with people in them*
*dangle a while in January blue //*


\*


If you live too many years far from your
roots they disappear & if you do not transplant there is
a sense of no

place     just

     float

Still a river city — but the river — broad, flat, crawling —
spells  *land-lock*
and no hilly prospect to look down upon it
or out above horizon   no
horizon

and no hills to undulate out there
    creating distance


plastic tangles in the currents

river as a blank upon an empty map    *fly-over country*


the Midwest South
malls picnic tables fried fish churches
on every corner   and motorcycles three abreast
golf smoke   dish drain   dry creeks

  biscuits   pig trucks   tobacco hats


by

water

        Ohio by

water bywater back
water by Oh
IO


northern mountains removed from the frame.

## A Story M tells Herself Begins:


*gutted*  :
not fish or deer    more like a building
the flashing yanked-out

pink stuff of insulation   – could kill you?  tiny particles that infiltrate
 a lung

 pink

   fibers ripped from where embedded


(can be
   blown in
to another wall/   walled-in   re-
placed:


<u>You have to remove the housing to get to the parts.</u>


                                        *how very White*
                                              *of you*

## Where She Fell

Thrust back in time through smudged polaroids
shadows in a box at Lyon's Lake
see mother in a sundress, turning washer-crank

the small troubled faces surimposed:  motherdaughter
before there was either

there was neither
& both


\*


Keep alert to
disappearing cadence:  up sleeves & inside the nose
under porch, barking   the snow
startled them

*no brakes at the top of the hill*

the club where she learned to smoke

wilting now in some
floorboard arrangement under peeling linoleum

cracker jacks with milk, coffee grounds suspended in a cup

the barking that frightened her

steps diminish in minor thirds

empty stomach like a socket or a tube, just waiting
*because that's where babies come from*

A moon shone off his gas-can
old guzzler, gussie, woods on either side & puzzled deer
sawed-off
& then while a night wind nippled
surface of the fussy water

it started up

began again:

so fields altered while pressed toward a lake bank
dizzy as gin, held back
the wicker fragments

(written on the back:   summer 1943)

## A Creek called Kinderhook:


swimsuit scraped
from skin   leaving a blank

concoction:  white, ripples
tar stains from cigarettes   or a distant
bruise

when it's wet it shrinks, you can hardly
get it off

*pressed*
*dyed cotton with*
*lake motif:  reflection, wavering*

## The Way It Tastes

One must leave many times in order to come back

– house in a state of perpetual rebuilding

Returns calculated against percentages of distance, rates falling

– as if something missing in M's body can only be recovered
in fields bordering a creek in Herkimer County

the older you get. a complicated
arithmetic: one friend from third grade times five plots in the Hebrew
    Farmers' cemetery

– fear of car won't start
bead dropping in an arc among fixed planets

multiply by stump of
a Dutch elm, throb inside a stubborn tooth.
No matter how the storefronts change, you know their insides.

– fitful house
that has banished the deer

\*

Ausable chasm.  ineluctable link
to some sheer flow through the floors of a hushed
museum: "the people of the State of New York":

– freezer full of them, dressed leather
fringe, designs against night sky

 Mr. fox  Mr. gray wolf (now extinct) and sweet fawn
a river's electronic lament

– the way a mouth tastes to itself when hungry
or in pain


the shaggy mastodons at the old museum with their yellow
yards' long tusks – little girls stare

– facts of ice underfoot
falling faster, rate per minute unmeasurable in white

*

how things smelled back then
fractions and blank windows   a long ruler's glide
through afternoons' February


unremarkable city on the banks of the Hudson:
home a sloop in the shape of a weathervane, the one that tops a bank
at the foot of Pearl Street


– across bridges, galloping ephemeron
lacks a head but carries its own grinning light

## Lament from The Scottish Borders

It's packed with mists  and the man sees Mary
   Queen of Scots riding after    her wounded lover

he sees a kind of light that makes
        the things it illumines    disappear

a light   oppositional

calls the past into the present in a way that
optically layers
so he views both yet   joins
neither

  the long-gone Reivers
            their pulse he feels trapped

within the
     forested  the centuried   light


      – conquered

he takes

photos of water
and the mist


a single white feather caught in wet grass


                cut-off

from a human  past

*

But what is  "going back"?

M gropes toward

– a river.
– a scrawl of smoke along a pane.
– a dock.
– a docked ship.


a bandage amid pines.  (always,
dark pines.)


Hudson's Half-Moon curled around
a golden lance, the four directions
bolted fast
to its shadow.


She says:
  – *Here at the cusp   where memory slips*
*I would feel friended again*
*by language*

invites     into her home the women     with their billowed aprons
    large hands

  the fathers
                    squinting beneath their beaver brims

One father, dying now
  his stomach distended
  drives around making a fond nuisance of himself
among his people:
store owners
barristas
the boy selling popcorn at the movies


he tells her:

*I've got to do this chemo again so I can*
*kick it out the door*


  Why shouldn't a man deny
the mortal facts?

          a native to his territory, he's entitled

to a hollow laugh.   —a man who claims the borders,
their summons   and

conspires

with shapes of light and moisture
brooding over empty hills.

## Paste This Country Over

the other:  by which M means
the lassitude of farmland, black fertile rows extending to
flat horizon, black barns cooking
tobacco leaf

Kentucky gets pasted in

over what grows dimmer
: dutch, pumpkins, hills, pines,
spines,

*I pine for you*
*over Norman's kill*, a kind of creek or river, or *hook*, the one

that holds you under
the bubbling surface

That smell, a northern one
crooked limestone teeth in cemeteries

where the names
have melted into tumulus
the hilly ground

\*

Over hollers and slit mountains
well-soaked trail of tears     Scotch-Irish lilt on fading faces
she wants to

paste it:  regions where the Iroquois confederated
naming stars after animal people

where the Dutch traded   constructing careful houses
tiled places to sleep
inside walls

in place of Ohio's muddy dirge *the knickerbockers*
*playing ninepins again*   (thunder's boom
vertiginous Hudson

the mountains where an old man slept off
a hundred years )

*Rensselaer  Stuyvesant*
words the web and net of our knowing

mind a tiny spider in
rafters of an aging barn

## A House in Which

what a ribbon
what a ribbon of event
what a furled  ribbon pulsing through


a house in which bodies shrank and burgeoned. fireplace burning old
newspapers and silence a clotting smoke. every year when winter loosed
its grip (though snow still lumped the streets and she jammed her knit
hat down for warmth) her lungs filled and she'd  have to leave her class-
room to cough in the high cold halls.

Nothing

happened here.  man rejected wife; brother menaced sister. girl
discovered pleasure between her legs.  dogs came and went. tests studied
for and passed, papers handed back, treasured comments in the margins.
one friend broke her arm. an old man keeled over. snowballs loaded with
ice pocked a girl's back and stung. blood and cramps garter belts and a
nightlight under its pink hood.      House

holding everything apart,      in place

*//  memoir meaning*

*hostility to sequence, strafing events to get at their illogic and yet*

                      *memory, remaking   : directionless, a snow*
*eclipsed by its sinking //*

                                       <u>How very white   of you</u>

# Right NowandThen

Tissue on slides:  the presence of incipient
malady.  place under microscope, change lenses
as necessary.

Varieties of this condition:

plagued by an awareness of 1967, 1963, etc. etc., spinning platters, Kodak
pictures, it's all out of order:
> *What difference does it make?* – her mother's weary
>> refrain

On good nights, his effusive half-ridicule:  food "cooked by Mama
> Elaine-o"

other times, his slashing disgust:  acrid mashed potatoes
dry steak

it's SHIT

> which brings us to:
>> DRECK (a ten-second play)

*This food is dreck your hair is dreck this house is dreck why can't you why can't she
why can't this it's all --*

(slam)


Coda:
– the woman named Elaine
flees upstairs & cries.

## House Scenes

Thick smells of chicken cavities stuffed with bunches
of tarragon & lemon ice-box cake   gold freckle, sprinkle on formica, a
kitchen to stir up hunger then lead it to cramped table in familiar
diagram:

details so important let's
run them again


:


Fluorescent lights batty in the kitchen.
white formica, gold flecks, simple white china or the kind
with pink roses, Rosenthal

Stabbing the meat with his fork —
low cloud ceiling, cigarette smoke

1967.

> *I sat next to her, yet*
> *facing him, remember nothing of her*
> *presence —*
> *my brother faced her, (perhaps it's why*
> *he married so young, gave her a grandchild?)*

Poor soldiers slathered in mud with reporter's mike thrust in their fake-
tough faces.


"The war in Southeast Asia
drags on…"

black & white Sony miniature perched atop a
counter providing backdrop to
consumption of canned green
beans, sumptuous pink roast


Just recalling
her mother's fingers especially, balancing
the cigarette

her Rob Roy, her Rusty Nail, apron bulging due to too many
of these, or cheese & triscuits when the dishes, done, enable her
to move to sofa in front of TV (not his chair)

*or am I conflating later images of her*
*divorced nights —*




        *// no one observes me.*
        *no child*
        *witnesses my doings*
        *keeps a journal, remembers years later, no*

        *I do it myself. //*




Do not forsake me, O my darling —
– his song.

Norm!!        *Leave her alone!*




                              or:
                              what about the time I was probably 6 or 7
she was holding me I was vomiting into the upstairs toilet but she had
trouble I was wriggling maybe throwing myself toward the open toilet
mouth she couldn't get hold of me I was scared I couldn't breathe maybe
I wasn't breathing she cried


N O R M !!    he came running upstairs and I don't remember what
happened exactly next except standing by the tub
his hand on my shoulder and he told me with great seriousness and calm
*You will always be able to breathe; you will never stop breathing* and I still
think of that if I start to panic maybe not throwing up but just in any
situation *I can breathe; I can always breathe*

MISSION

*Accomplished*

THE STORY OF THE XXIX TAC

## Saturday Night

M's fixing her dinner, she has the house to herself, it's
pigs in blankets (tiny kosher hotdogs wrapped in *treyf* refrigerator dough).
She nests upstairs in her room with its poster of Zeffirelli's Romeo and Juliet,
this place where she's always reading, while her younger brother's out
or otherwise invisible        no —
she's invisible.

The way she likes it.

Redux:

## A NIGHT OUT AT THE CLUB

(It's the Jewish country club — the one built in modern splendor when
the *goyim* wouldn't let us into the old manse on the golf course west of town)

The woman prepares:

— her swingin' earrings: little disco balls suspended
by silvery links
— her lipstick: Sea Coral or Yardley Pink
— her hair: cut '60s short with mod bangs
— her skin: tan
— her body: thick
— her smile: hopeful
— her daughter: watching, collecting
— her age: *it's 1967 & when she died in '89 she was 69 and this
is always how I do the math. Forty-seven so he's 43*
— his comment

YOU LOOK LIKE _____

& turns, bang! out the back kitchen door

& feet run upstairs, high heels shed on carpet

hand over mouth stifled sobs

This could be Lana Turner playing to whichever man was nasty to her next
except Lana was a piece of work

let's run it through again:  *take!*

  exists now only in M's head

principals, dead
& family dog

bonemeal in the yard

secondary character —
son, "watching TV" who claims non-memory


yes, both principals now

bonemeal *& this story I tell myself under*
          *bone-lid —*

## Passing Away

Twenty-two years after she goes (lung cancer) it's his
turn (the prostate)

– winds up ash inside a box in brother's closet


Recall:
how efficiently the adult children dismantled every
trace — cabinets
spilled into gaping cardboard, clothes to Goodwill bed to hospice photos
divvied into piles, shoved in manila envelopes still awaiting
collection

– every single thing fingered & assigned its fate
trash bags swelled fat

M lost count after a few days —
the music in the walls set to that soothing station


They had waited for him to pass
with some impatience.

His empty
body, the first thing out the door.


The house sold six weeks later.

## The P-47 Pilot

At last, his most Russian
  face, big-nosed, high-cheeked, unlined as a boy's

impervious to M's final
conversation

the nurse lets her move the stethoscope over
his bare chest
  30 minutes after it was called


M thinks:

*// poetry anarchic goes free in a culture*
*where everything's priced, exchanged for*
 *"value" //*


     therefore any written ending must be

provisional

    imposed

(because humans sometimes need a sense of

   arrival)

*

To become that shell or shield that moves back across
Atlanta Hartfield with its streaming lights
at a glance not possible


yet     to be lifted silver   a thing bulging
with packed personal items

we need a frame: constraint

    something to say "mission accomplished"
       to record touchdowns and ports of call in
            "serviceman's diary"




but does poetry ever     arrive?
   no eagle, its motion a river
dragging limbs & deer parts,     oil cans
          coke bottles burger boxes eternal
    plastic mesh


   – everything that passes, it collects   *stuccoed o'er*
as Whitman said

       a flume
    to fertilize the territory with its
                              departure

\*

imagine: a view of the beloved earth
under-wing 70 years back, the bombs
giddy screech across German
   sky


that craft yanked
   flaming down by his keen training  only 18
*hot shot*


  yet never to see the faces (maybe just once —
*looked straight at each other then it was*
  *see ya!*



and all the semen bedded between the cold
blonde thighs,
   gone


  and the children's children and their children

   *passed by censor for mailing home*

\*

*Eyes rolled up, he dreams*:

radio transmission from Ninth Army:  <u>Boy, how we love you guys</u>


    when the air came in

rain squalls
    *Tactical Air Command*

pouring ruin on the Ruhr


        arrowing from the skies   600-foot ceiling

*right where we want'em*


        Mustang and Lightning reconnaissance
first beat the brush, photographed the maze, then the P-47s

        smoke-eaters

        lush targets

only so many synonyms for *smashed*
factories . transports . platoons

P-47s
        clearing hills and trees by 50 feet to reach

           right into the gun pits

           heart of the Fatherland


    Survivors fled to the woods (the classic
gesture)

the rip, the mournful *kriye*


kept open till this      last death

*

Sheer-fire ran them first        over the Rhine:

this was his medaled memory.


        When the breathing stopped her father looked —
alive


and poetry
        an under-mire:


an old scarlet unlikely to linger

    or guide him wheels down across the future


Still —
everything becomes a memory the moment after
you think it.

                                *What difference does it make?*


— the books exploding toward us   shelf upon shelf

# Women's Pictures

## And Other Fairytales

The Dharma teacher says:

   "You condition yourself to being the
person you are"

*Happiness:  a cocktail umbrella*
*over my head*

*

Up from the disheveled cloths of sleep at 4 am as if
headed toward the airport
(yet nowhere
to go)

she:  stepping out from the letter M
     the letter becoming
her sign

Truncated legs, feathers   bursting out of
her back, she's a torn-open
pillow
(every Jewish family has its story:  sabers, cats and
pregnant bellies)
– did some Cossack?
                    *no* –


She simply exposes herself, nulliparous


to possible flight.

\*

Alberta clipper
slicing into Louisville furnace

the smell of things burning:

    rubber tires, a skim of oil bobbing on the river, the scorch
given off by melting plastics

wind whisks & tree branch
  taps — taps       her roof
                        *& rupture?*

wind   50 mph gusts

— the section above M's bed,  that
safest most protected place.
could it stab through?
                she hopes it does.

\*

*This moment* with its bilious green
swollen leafing knocked

hollow, milky fuzz       tufting      out.  Bound

to another landscape   *Poylish*
its heritage : blood

as in   the buzz above a darkened piece of earth
supressing other sound   the sun   a cotton-edge of hills   *running*

its after.  math.



A geography does not exist unless
she invests it with meaning.

*

The body collects, grows its own flowers.

Each woman looks out from a big frame

house, boiling with words
no one in that upstate town could understand

Words    learned inside another house
with a dirt floor by the Dnieper

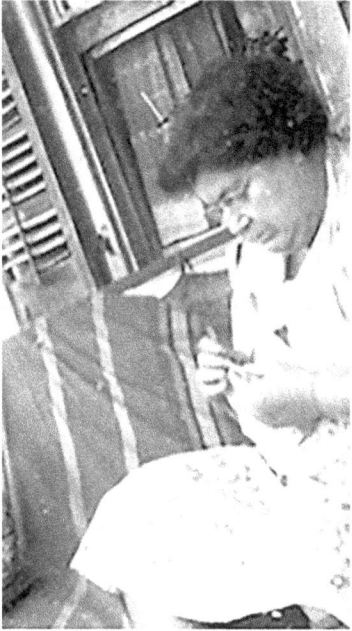

warm grassy hills outside Albany where wind makes a path

garden's clumps in nose-singeing heat

woman selling eggs from the back of a truck
mending shirts on a dirty porch:  a tale

to frighten children, never told.

What is it that
stops memory?   before/          after

Is culture transplantable like potatoes?

*Never told, never unfolded*

instead, little Golden Books, early Disney, dream archery
a girl opens her lips and lets fall pearls and roses and

insects, pebbles, toads

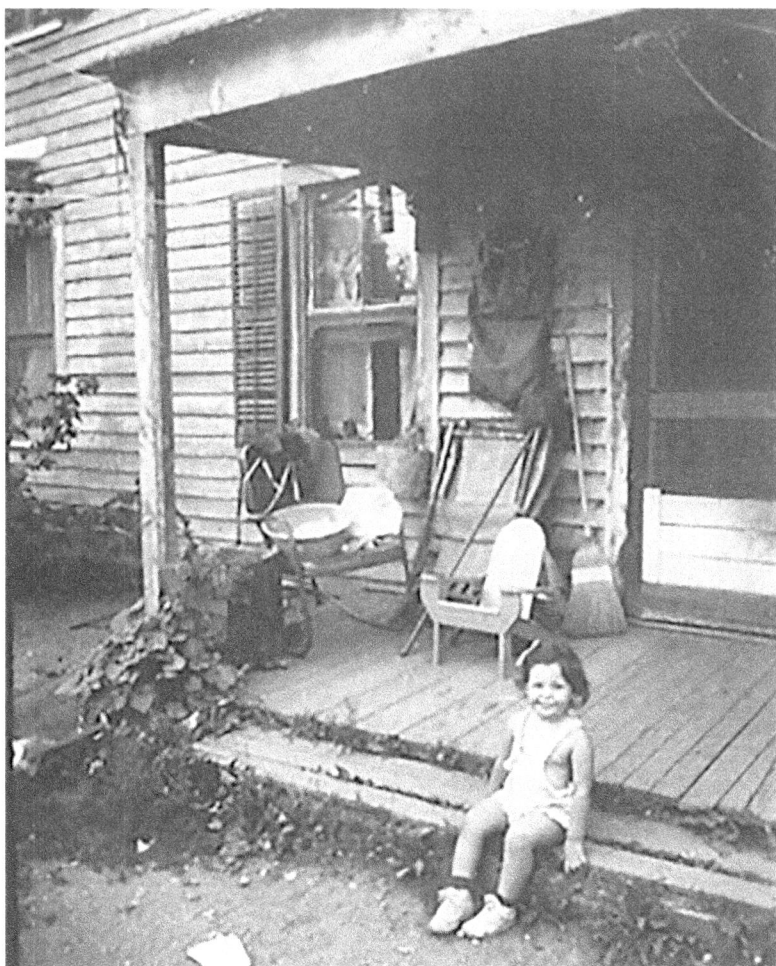

# dream

widows, orphans
those irregular letters
cut from the fringe of the field


at night a pasture opens before her.  ice skates, her feet trimmed with
rabbit fur. they add an extra ten feet of dirt, then allow houses to be
built, roads paved over the burials.


\*


remember

   enclosures?  under whose legs, or body pressing down in the way-back
   yard under the dried and tangled leaves.  a sense of
   cheating, or just lying, a guilty feeling taken into the room with the
   shiny

   tables, the book bag, waxed apple. hiding under the desk in the drills
   made you feel the opposite
   of safe, its little wooden house your shelter

   *it slittle*

   *its slit*

## And Other Pictures

Does brother remember? M does: their childish difference concentrated
in front of the TV for a black & white movie they're
commanded to watch, a thing called   *Night and Fog*

bodies turned limp and stringy scooped
out of pits with the heads flung back
mouths gaping

Who is more silent?
they sit in a hush.


Brother, sister, *look* the parents seem to say
  what they did to the Jews
not so long ago
close enough to feel the thrill of fear


– and yet M never saw a number inked on
anyone's arm, growing up

just a fact becoming a fable, a legend of the Jews –
skin for lampshades & hair-filled rooms


and millions of empty shoes.

## Their Women-Bodies

those women uniformly thick   ribbed stockings (black line darting up
to a secret place)   mouths wise   red smeared a little   glasses   smiling, nostrils
exhaling smoke

they knew


a thing of *flanken*   chicken legs spread
scoop out the stuff, kidney liver heart
savory juices leaking on the dish

*gehakte lebn*   lots of *shmaltz*   and angel food sponge to drift
along a tongue


laughter deep in throat    hands reaching down, rough   with nails

polished     the woman-bodies &

the girl

watchful

    watching

*//When you think everything written can be*

*betrayal yet the way one receives*

*these myriad impressions the only way to piece*

*together this diminished*

*history//*


What difference does it make?

<u>How very white of you</u>

# M

## The Woman Without Experiences

travels the length
of a penstroke, her breath
occluded in a fringe of sunlight

passage of Canada geese over the reservoir
their calls woke her this morning
that much is real

as real as mice scratching inside a winter-wall
or a window's revelation of misshapen leaves--
furled bats hanging in evening darkness

*

Strange: there is no doubt she has lived
through several decades from Jackie Kennedy's
blood-splashed hat

shelves of journals record the interior life of
the girl-body: its moods, encounters as chemicals shook
her insides with fuming abundance & pulled the blood
into the low-down pocket

yet the woman can wander
her rented rooms & in each one
forget a little more

except

        the vivid way she stands, at 30
next to her present self     the one she barely recognizes

whose reflections no longer mirror the person
she understood herself to be


She recalls:
a figure sprinting nightly through labyrinths beneath
a city's spread

  This was M
       trying to make a late train across San Francisco Bay

while painfully missing the man at the other edge – New York –
his patient turning of pages
his perch above a street, rat-infested

where paints control the light
and a rusted tank sends dirty water to the river

tub pitched in the kitchen
a bed of moldy tee shirts,
confusion marked by joking
under the sheets

       stand-in for love

## Some Experiences

1.  Small stitches of hammock rows, bothering corn

2.  A funnel chased them to the mall, the wavery siren falling chunks of ice

3.  Thai pepper burning insides of the lips

4.  A woman planning for a baby, she has the name picked out, will fly 9,000 miles to get her

5.  Where the wind dies down, smoke rises keen and cold enough to see your breath, mornings

6.  Hunted by owls

7.  Another place — breathless after short walks and smelling mountain lion piss on stumps


In 15 months she moved five times.
Illinois, Iowa — just so much static.
Pick up suitcase, stuff it in the back seat.  Leave expensive
shampoo in Nebraska where the "healthy meal" was canned
vegetables, coated in butter.

Sun knocked her right side
for days — and what did she not leave in
Colorado?  She did not leave bits of soap, did not steal

the ashtrays.  Calling from a payphone next to a real stuffed bobcat
in a large display case somewhere in Nevada.  Oh yes it snowed
as they headed over the pass that June day —


only to arrive in a place of no rivers
attached to a watery edge
dunked in fog

living trellis of ants in the kitchen, ascending a pail

No rivers — did I say that?  to match a body's veins?

Just a drop-off into ocean to sail away and never be seen
again.

# San Francisco

A view from the cheap seats:  how did the Mission taste,
in fog?  the boys' giggles, wavering down Valencia
arms around each other

    How they studied their moves in studio mirrors – triplet steps,
*jetés*   until touched by wands they shrank

into little old men with barking coughs & lesions.
(the sand left by a body
she stuck her hands in, helped to scatter
in slopping waves    )

Each scene bears seeds of its perpetuation
memory now understood to be radioactive
a poison    she once thought kept her    alive

                *How very*
                    *Very white of you*

# Suggestions from the Dharma Teacher

Pretend you can unzip your body and lift out its organs
one by one.  As you examine your liver, ask: *Am I this liver?*
As you reveal your left lung, ask: *Am I this lung?*
Am I this eyeball? this sheath of fat?

And so on.

Look into the mirror, into your own eyes, for fifteen minutes.
Ask: *Who is looking?*
*Who is being seen?*

Recall twenty of the times you were most happy in your life.

*Where are they now?*

## Behold:

the body with its moving parts, its various separate lives.

A material called: "felt."
Elmer's we used to glue,
bring the spangles to the paper, press them on, a mess.
a floury scum on the table: aftermath
of pastry.
Smoke rising from her cigarette
fumes rising from the sink, bleach.

Fingers knobbly, skin withered.
oh, in the general sadness, raise your arms, lift them
*up! up!*
to stop a cough. And she pats your back, soundly.

## AlbanyNewYork

Lew & Mary's sealed-up apartment on a street with a bird name,
their table a narrow space of dingy white – clotted lace –
where they sat picking at herring & pieces of washed-out milky iceberg
    lettuce

in Albany
the year before her mother died

but Lew, of course, went first
surrendering his gold regalia   the watch & rings, the bling
he favored
   and blue shivering hands

and her mother in a morphine dream
  saw him from her hospital bed
months after his burial

Some years before
   it was
  Izzie, Nate and Jenny

Roselee and David    a few years after

M keeps track.

Behold:

organs on the ultrasound — a silent crowd.
they can't even find the pancreas
half the time. "Does it look happy?" she wants
to know. "Oh yes it does" – in there,
inside the sack
where invisible blood careens around
with never occasion
to stop

*

*his brow against my shoulder, mine against his chest, his against my thigh*

*a dream begins inside one head, transfers itself intact into another*

waking suddenly because
her body's turning over a mile
of cells —
thickening, gathering stitches, laying in extra stock then
   letting out the pattern, softened yarn.

## Children

He was the dark one.  Saw his father whip his
mother with the gun.  He liked to say <u>My daddy's
gonna shoot you</u>, if you got tired of tossing the ball
back and forth.  When he smiled it was a knife
slicing an orange, the sweet juice splattered you.


\*


"I agree it's weird," said the woman called sister-in-law,
standing back turned to M, arms sunk elbow-deep in a sink of dirty dishes.

"No I didn't mean it's weird not to want them," M said, "but
to have decided like this"


Not to want the baby pulp wrapped in a blanket
the helpless head tipped back, eyes sealed in sleep
breath making its first purple marks under
thin veil of skin. Blood shaping its migration through
delicate pockets only recently
stitched shut


not


to want a blossom so tender that touch leaves faint
indentations. The ancient obligations: taste of milk


Into that swaddling in your arms the person
grows – light years off.

Now, everything waits

for the royal germ to be planted inside the slippery coat


Blankets = fill.
Bellies = swell.
Breasts = fatten.


(but if the queen

should decline —  ?)

## That Summer

In the supple mooring of her body afloat
a Canadian lake
adrift toward the far shore, mottled and distorted

she'd never thought how quickly it takes place
takes   her place

the place of

her body afloat
a fray
a dragging


*


Working it out in pencil on
the back of a board
how much the cost: bicuspid   biscuit   purple stain
where the IV goes in

for flesh to make its
statement: adjudication: puncture: "I am here"  "here?"

a gallery of answers   no one
pays any
mind

*

a festering among pines

a lake's skin


"being" :

                       a fusing of the body
                     & mind   (its foam or
froth at the crest

   waves encircle the nucleus
icy tumultuous jade

   the froth pounded into existence
hisses
sucked back

   back & forth


You can
lift the spine of a trout entire
from its braid of flesh
toss it out


*How lightly embedded*
  *we are*

\*

Still:

there must be a strict
discipline to grief

only the drip of a regulated dose
only the briefest
flash of an aperture

to contain

a void

in the space of a musical measure


a loneness a puzzle.
a fact to drape
a life around.

## California Again

Backyards there    a tangle of shed
growth, pierced
by terrific pinks, violets    no wall or shut
door is not permeable

to ants   their moist successions.
It's wet: stick a finger in    mix with it.

Pieces of darkened petals   their once-clean shapes
  altered
  carried off

Pry open the lids   (even if to expose

  traps

       the mouths   floating

       waiting   to be fed )

*

So many pages scribbled over, fake attempts to
"get it all down" as if
one could report at the scene    of living:

for example
white ridges:    could be snow
  or a backbone
under parchment

*

 "Brooding"    the word always

reminds her of its cousins in sound, *ruby, brook,* flashing
through an invented
darkness.

*vos iz faran,* what exists, *iz* —

          how the words choke up, earth thrown down
on them (kindness at an open
grave).
Here are the impermissions:

do not speak, the words are dead.
do not stitch into a complex form.
do not say "I" ("I") *I* —

*Space is just the externalization of what you really are.*

*

How a superficial
wound heals, gathering
clumps of alien skin.


The arteries    interrogatory

decisions worked through cellular

openings like yarn


through a burlap picture.
Embroidery kit:

knitting the fat blanched clusters
all night.

## That Summer

Lungs swelled with purpose

  a drastic color against brick


tightrope walker trembling above flagstones
  high inside the vault
of a dim cathedral


To live requires restraint
  a kind of violence


*// New York inside my body*

*sleepwalking toward Morningside Park //*

# ThenandNow

How warm and careful it feels
to slide into bed beside a sleeping cat
a Chagall angel tacked fluttering to the lilac wall.

*In the event we should lose power*
*the lights will guide you*
*to the nearest exit.*

*Just follow the strips*
*the lighted pathways* — up the hillside in damp
March darkness

where ghosts have penetrated
up through stony earth, rotted floorboards

They will be joining you soon.

\*

To reassure you:
that sink of dirty dishes you left
will be here in the morning
you can count on that

but the sun on your cheek through the window overlooking
an Oakland garden
will not

nor will the garden exist nor
the window or even the shadow
of the man who stood beside you, the one
called "husband," looking out

nor even the woman
you think
or thought
  you were.

# Catching Up with the Ancestors

She drives to work, a tiny bit of her leg
in a plastic cup

extracted, a shiny lump
of cells to be examined & proclaimed
Yea,
   Nay.

Next week she'll leave two tubes of blood
in a basement lab called Quest.

The quest:  to be punctuated
      with *waking*

  no algorithm for this

though she's jealous of science and its grid of inquiry
the logical progression
from hypothesis to test    to diagnosis to
conclusion.

\*

Diagnosis:   Sap fails to rise
treatment:   there is none.

still:  scratching, the letters
twist inside her arm, the leg, incise themselves
beneath the skin to be read

on the surface:
ligature
 scrawl
   nothing
simple as a line


still:  can't get used to
seeing the inverse of things:


mirror to this ivory ghost

the dis-
enchantment:    seeing one's
self locked
a figure in the carpet

     left for several centuries in lurid fibrous dark


But isn't that
  *this* moment
without insight?

# Violet

— the color of summer dusks circa

1960
>> humidity pierced by the scent of downed
>> pine needles and children's

cries tearing through backyards

>> rampant

>> fireflies fly


In memory's gauze :

>> a woman smiling     hands still in gardening gloves
clasping a pink glass
>> rattle of ice

her white polo shirt turning whiter as the evening slowly
  darkens


A man's voice, cutting through

*children,     time for bed*   my

mother's
          body freckled
                              peach a favored

    pair of gardening shorts    & the smoke
Tareytons
          ( my father's   Lucky Strikes )




*what difference does it make?*
                        her frustration
                                          if I dawdled amid choices
banana or apple
          blue shirt   yellow


now sums up
what memory means when the film

                        plays forward

still:
      I keep them both
          inside a single night of summer


under Arcturus —
      bulge of light in dilute sky


adjacent
  to wandering ants     tucked in folds of
        peony


                 Here and now

in a position neither origin nor destination, just
a place


where the river's broad & wrinkled as skin
      translucent yet


filled with trash, undigested, spewed-up
          on a jeweled edge

mother

        father

        you left behind the same words:

scribbled in day books   planners     sifted among

  doctors' appointments

     *morphine*

*pain worse*
                    *could not*

                         *sleep*


look:    I have converted you to

# Notes

The questions that appear on p.10 ("Questions for My Russian Grandmother") are quoted, with a few alterations, from Nathaniel Deutsch's translation of Sh. Ansky's "Jewish Ethnographic Program" (*The Jewish Dark Continent: Life and Death in the Russian Pale of Settlement,* Harvard University Press, 2011; p 107, 111, 113, 114.)

Two of the films referenced in the section *Women's Pictures — Magnificent Obsession* (1954) and *Imitation of Life* (1959) — were directed by Douglas Sirk. *Now Voyager* (1942) was directed by Irving Rapper.

The poem "Lament from The Scottish Borders" refers to the Scottish film artist Richard Ashrowan and materials in his monograph *Lament* (Nowhere Arts, 2009).

www.ingramcontent.com/pod-product-compliance
Lightning Source LLC
Chambersburg PA
CBHW022200080426
42734CB00006B/516